Taj Mahal

MIKAYA PRESS

NEW YORK

FOR LUCAS AND OTTAVIA

Author's Note

Researching and writing this book would not have been possible without the help of scholars who have devoted decades to the study of the Taj Mahal and the magnificent Mughals who built it.

The author wishes to thank:

Elizabeth B. Moynihan, author of The Moonlight Garden *and* Paradise As A Garden, *for her invaluable critique of the manuscript and Dr. D. Dayalan, Superintending Archaeologist, Archaeological Survey of India, Agra, for hours of enlightening conversation, and for reading and commenting on the manuscript. The book would be poorer without their efforts.*
All errors of fact and interpretation are mine alone.
Thanks also to Dr. R.K. Dixit, Senior Conservation Assistant, Archaeological Survey of India, Agra, for graciously sharing his time and expertise, and to Benoy K. Behl, Dr. Ebba Koch, and Dr. James L. Westcoat, Jr. for insight, encouragement and help.

Books by Elizabeth Mann
The Brooklyn Bridge
The Great Pyramid
The Great Wall
The Roman Colosseum
The Panama Canal
Machu Picchu
Hoover Dam
Tikal
Empire State Building
The Parthenon

Editor: Stuart Waldman
Design: Lesley Ehlers Design
Copyright © 2008 Mikaya Press
Illustrations Copyright © Alan Witschonke
Map Copyright © Jane Shasky

Library of Congress Cataloging-in-Publication Data

Mann, Elizabeth, 1948-
Taj Mahal / by Elizabeth Mann ; with illustrations by Alan Witschonke.
p. cm. — (A wonders of the world book)
Includes bibliographical references and index.
ISBN 1-931414-20-3
1. Taj Mahal (Agra, India) 2. Mogul Empire—Kings and rulers. I. Witschonke, Alan, 1953- II. Title.
DS486.A3M36 2008
954.02'57092—dc22
                        2008060054

Printed in China

Taj Mahal

A WONDERS OF THE WORLD BOOK

BY ELIZABETH MANN

WITH ILLUSTRATIONS BY ALAN WITSCHONKE

MIKAYA PRESS

NEW YORK

Prince Khurram was fifteen years old when he fell in love. The fourteen year old who captured his heart was as bright and generous as she was beautiful. Four years later, in 1612, they were married. From that day on, Mumtaz Mahal was his constant companion, his trusted advisor, the love of his life. In the Muslim world, where arranged marriages were customary and men were allowed four wives, such devotion to one woman was unusual. She was at his side when he became the emperor of the Mughal Empire and took the title Shah Jahan (World Ruler), and she was at his side when he led armies against rebels in remote and dangerous areas.

In 1631 she went with him on a military campaign to a region called the Deccan, far from their palace in Agra. The campaign promised to be long, so the royal court, including the women who attended Mumtaz Mahal, moved to the Deccan with the emperor and his army. Near the town of Burhanpur, they set up a city of tents where life went on much as it had in the palace while the army skirmished with the enemy.

In the hot month of June, the mood in the zanana (women's quarters) was tense and excited. Mumtaz Mahal was about to give birth to her 14th child! One night she dreamed that she heard her unborn baby cry. When she told her women about it, tension became fear. Such a dream was a bad omen.

At last the infant was born, and fear turned to joy—the baby girl was healthy. At the sight of the weakened queen lying exhausted against her silken cushions, joy quickly faded. Fearing the worst, Mumtaz Mahal summoned Shah Jahan to her tent. She asked only that he care for her children and then died in his arms.

The emperor was devastated. He wept for a week, and it is said that the hair of his beard turned white. He put aside the silk clothing and bright jewels that he had worn all his life and dressed instead in white mourning clothes. He turned away from music, dance, all entertainment. Nothing gave him pleasure.

Despite his grief, Shah Jahan was not one to neglect his duties as emperor. He rose at dawn to pray in the tiny mosque in his palace and then took his place in the throne room. He listened patiently as nobles and commoners alike approached him with their problems and requests. He rewarded those who pleased him with gifts of jewels, elephants, and land. For the unlucky, executioners were on hand to carry out swift punishments. Day after day, he forced himself to perform the routines of the imperial court.

The only light for Shah Jahan in this time of darkness was his plan to build a tomb for Mumtaz Mahal. This work he embraced eagerly. He wanted to create a paradise for his great queen, and a monument to their love. Thus from the emperor's grief the Taj Mahal was born.

This sad and romantic tale is as well-known as the Taj Mahal itself. It has been repeated for centuries by people all over the world. But the story of the Taj Mahal is larger, wilder, and more complicated.

It begins in the tiny kingdom of Ferghana in the mountains of Central Asia. There, in 1483, a warlord was tending his pigeons in their roost that sat high on the wall of his fortress. Suddenly the ancient wall crumbled, and the roost toppled down. The pigeons escaped to freedom; the warlord fell to his death. His son Babur, just 11 years old, became the ruler of Ferghana. Rival warlords planned their attacks. An army led by a child seemed an easy conquest, but Babur was not an ordinary child.

Babur was descended from two of the greatest conquerors the world had ever known, the Mongol tribal leader Chinghis Khan and the Muslim Turk Timur. In the 1200s, Chinghis Khan and his horsemen built an empire that stretched from the Pacific Ocean across Asia to Europe, and south to the Indus River in Hindustan (India). In the 1300s, Timur conquered most of Central Asia, then went on to plunder northern Hindustan.

With the blood of these two legendary warriors in his veins, Babur did not lack courage and ambition, but the enemies who surrounded him were powerful. After years of fighting, he had lost Ferghana and could only claim the city of Kabul and a small army as his own. He realized that his dreams of conquest were not going to come true in Central Asia. Like Chingis Khan and Timur before him, he looked toward wealthy Hindustan. Perhaps there he could make his fortune.

In 1526 he led 12,000 followers over the rugged Hindu Kush mountains and on to the same wide plains in northern Hindustan that Timur had ravaged over a century earlier. On February 19, at a place called Panipat, he found an army of 100,000 men and 1,000 elephants waiting to challenge him. It was a frightening sight, but Babur's soldiers were tough, disciplined and experienced. Most important, they had guns. By midday the bloody battle was over. Babur moved his court to the city of Agra and claimed it as his capital. The Mughal Empire, whose name comes from the word Mongol, was born. Babur was its first emperor.

During his short reign, from 1526 to 1530, Babur established the Mughal Empire and set an example for his descendants who would rule for generations to come.

Humayun took the throne in 1530 and struggled to hang on to it until his death in 1556. He did not have his father's talent for war, and his superstitions often led him to make bad military decisions.

One of Babur's first acts as emperor was to build a large garden, a *charbagh*, on the banks of the Yamuna River in Agra. Garden-building might seem an unusual activity for a conquering warrior, but for Babur it was a natural thing to do. He had inherited more than a talent for war from his famous ancestors.

Chinghis Khan, a nomad, spent his life outdoors. Timur created *charbaghs* so beautiful they were called "paradise gardens." Both men had a deep love of nature and Babur had inherited that, too. In Kabul he had chosen to live outdoors in a tent among the sights, sounds, and smells of his own peaceful, well-tended *charbagh*. He intended to do the same in Hindustan.

The new *charbagh* must have truly seemed like a paradise to the homesick emperor. Cool and leafy as his garden in Kabul, it gave him welcome relief from the unrelenting heat and dust of of his new home. Nobles and wealthy landowners, eager to please the new ruler, followed his example, and soon splendid *charbaghs* lined both sides of the Yamuna.

Akbar's taste for conquest led him to many military successes during his reign from 1556 to 1605. He strengthened Mughal control in distant regions. He was known for welcoming all religions in his court.

Jahangir's reign, from 1605 to 1627, did not begin until he was nearly 40 years old. He trained for the job by leading his father's armies into battle.

Babur had little time to enjoy his lovely *charbagh*. He died in 1530, four years after the victory at Panipat.

His son Humayun succeeded him, but he lost control of the empire. His enemies, including three of his brothers who wanted to replace him as emperor, drove him out of Hindustan in 1540. Humayun battled for 15 years and at last regained the throne in 1555. Seven months later he fell on the steps of his library and died of his injuries. It was left to his 13-year-old son Akbar to restore greatness to the still-shaky Mughal Empire.

Akbar did just that. In the 49 years of his reign, his conquests pushed the Mughal borders in every direction. When Akbar, whose name means "The Great," died in 1605, he left a vast and powerful empire to his son Jahangir.

During the 22 years that he ruled, Jahangir managed to hold the territory conquered by Akbar, but it was a difficult task. Rebellions in different parts of Hindustan kept his armies constantly on the move.

All together, Babur, Humayun, Akbar, and Jahangir ruled for nearly 100 years. It was an unsettled, war-torn century, and they faced challenges away from the battlefield as well.

The Mughals were foreigners in the land they had conquered. They were also Muslims, where most of their subjects were Hindus. Hindus worshiped many gods; Muslims worshiped one. Hindus believed cows were sacred; Muslims ate beef. Hindus cremated their dead; Muslims buried theirs. The differences were great, and could have led to conflict within the empire.

The Mughals were not about to let religious differences interfere with building an empire. They appointed Hindus to important government positions and adopted Hindu traditions. They married Hindu wives and hired Hindu artists and workers.

Such diplomacy, backed up by powerful armies, served these brilliant emperors well. They created an empire second only to that of the great Ming Empire in China. The Mughals ruled 150 million people, a quarter of the world's population.

Their subjects grew crops and raised livestock on millions of acres of fertile land. They used centuries-old skills to weave fine fabrics and carpets. They made jewelry, pots, sandals and many other useful and beautiful things. By collecting taxes on everything that was produced in Hindustan, the Mughals became the richest people in the world. Their wealth was staggering, spectacular, uncountable.

The Mughal Empire once included most of what is today India, Pakistan, Bangladesh, and Afghanistan.

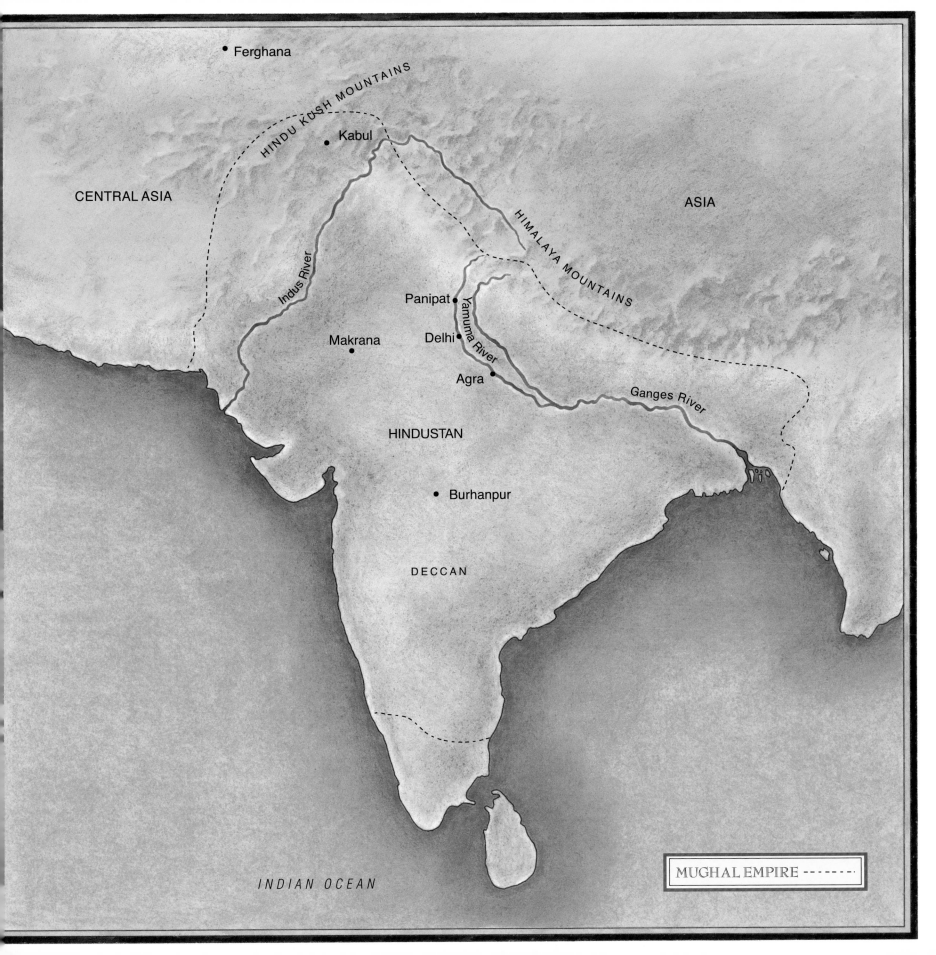

Ferghana

HINDU KUSH MOUNTAINS

CENTRAL ASIA

Kabul

ASIA

Indus River

HIMALAYA MOUNTAINS

Panipat

Yamuna River

Makrana

Delhi

Agra

Ganges River

HINDUSTAN

Burhanpur

DECCAN

INDIAN OCEAN

MUGHAL EMPIRE - - - - - - -

The Mughals lived in eye-popping splendor, spending their great fortune in spectacular ways. They reclined on soft carpets and embroidered cushions wearing silken trousers and vests studded with gems. Ropes of pearls hung from their necks and jewels sparkled on thumbs, toes and turbans. At mealtime fifty different dishes were prepared and served on plates of gold, silver, and white jade while dancers and musicians performed.

Like their nomadic Mongol ancestors, the Mughals were often on the move. They traveled throughout the empire, for war and for pleasure, and they made sure that even their most luxurious belongings traveled as easily as they did. Carpets and tents, silk robes and cushions, gems and pearls all were portable. The entire contents of a royal chamber could be piled on the back of an elephant and re-created in whatever fort or garden the wandering emperor chose.

The most ordinary objects of daily life were transformed into works of art for the Mughal emperors. This priceless spoon, used by the emperor Akbar, is made of gold and set with rubies, emeralds, and diamonds.

The Mughals were also deeply interested in literature and art. They created a number of unique books that are still read and marveled at.

It began with Babur, who kept a journal of his life in Central Asia and continued it during his reign in Hindustan. He described everything from his favorite melons to prisoner executions. The *Baburnama* (Book of Babur) inspired his descendants to record their lives and reigns also.

Talented artists illustrated the emperors' journals, creating some of the most beautiful artwork of the Mughal era. The paintings, always small enough to be bound into books for travel, still exist today. The bright colors and rich details provide a look back into the strange and magnificent life of the Mughals.

Eight fingers were not enough to display a Mughal emperor's finery—they had rings made for their thumbs as well. This one is jewelled inside and out.

Charbaghs *were important to Babur, and he mentions them often in the* Baburnama. *Here the emperor, in yellow, is supervising his gardeners as they measure out flower beds in one of them. Like all Babur's* charbaghs, *this one is a square surrounded by a high wall. The streams and plants are arranged in squares also.*

Akbar, like all Mughal emperors, was fond of violent entertainment. He often staged elephant fights. Priceless animals were goaded to fight, sometimes to the death, during thunderous battles, like this one shown in the Akbarnama.

Mughal hunting expeditions like the one shown here in the Akbarnama lasted for weeks, and involved thousands of people, hundreds of elephants, and trained hunting cheetahs. A cheetah would chase down a deer, return dragging the kill, then settle on a carpet to await the choice morsels of meat that were its reward. The cheetah (center) wears a jeweled collar fit for an emperor.

Mughals could be very generous. In this painting from the Jahangirnama *young Prince Khurram (who later became Shah Jahan) is seated on one side of a scale; bags of gold and silver are stacked on the other side. When the scales balanced, Jahangir gave away his son's weight in silver and gold to the poor.*

The daggers, knives, and gold cups on display in front of the scale, as well as the scale itself, are encrusted with precious jewels.

The Mughals were also generous to courtiers and nobles, but they expected generosity from them in return. This painting is from the Padshahnama, *the record of Shah Jahan's reign. It shows the sumptuous gifts being brought to the wedding of Shah Jahan's favorite son, Dara Shukoh.*

As the empire grew larger and wealthier, the emperors' extravagance increased. Each ruler outdid his father, and everything from hunting expeditions to turban jewels became more lavish and costly. Even death became extravagant.

When Babur died in 1530, he was buried according to Muslim law in a grave marked only with a mound of earth. By the time of his son Humayun's death, 26 years later, such a commonplace burial was unthinkable. Humayun was laid to rest in the center of a beautiful *charbagh* in a large mausoleum (tomb building) made of red sandstone. And his son Akbar's burial 50 years later was even grander.

At the end of the first century of Mughal rule in late 1627, the fourth emperor Jahangir died after a long illness. Shah Jahan was his chosen successor, but rivals wanted to rule in his place.

Shah Jahan left nothing to chance. Even before his father fell ill, he began clearing a path to the throne. By the time he took his place as the fifth Mughal emperor on January 21, 1628, there was no one left to challenge him. Three of his brothers, two young nephews, and two cousins were dead. Some died of mysterious causes; most were murdered on his orders.

The Mughals were no strangers to violence—it was how they got what they wanted—but Shah Jahan's crimes against his family were brutal even by their standards. The time would come when he would feel the terrible consequences of his actions, but in 1628 his deeds were never questioned—he had the power of life and death over anyone who dared to criticize him. In fact, the early years of his reign appeared to be the happiest of his life. He had the riches of the world at his feet and his beloved Mumtaz Mahal at his side.

Just four years later he was planning her burial.

During his reign from 1628 to 1658, Shah Jahan took Mughal spending to great heights. The emperor was an enthusiastic architect and lavished money on elaborate building projects. He loved gems, and was an expert judge of quality. It's said that he kept bowls of diamonds, emeralds, and rubies nearby during meals to offer to his guests.

The idea for his wife's tomb began as a simple expression of love and grief, but in true Mughal fashion it became very large and grand. Of all the emperors, Shah Jahan was the one who most enjoyed displaying his riches. The tomb would give him a chance to dazzle the world. He turned his attention, and the wealth and talent of the empire, to the Taj Mahal.

Shah Jahan chose a site for Mumtaz Mahal's burial *charbagh* a mile downriver from his palace in the Agra Fort. More than forty *charbaghs* had been built along the Yamuna since Babur's time, but Mumtaz Mahal's would dwarf them all. The mausoleum would be the first Mughal tomb built for a woman, and it would be the biggest one ever.

The *charbagh* and mausoleum were to be part of an even larger complex of courtyards, gardens, and buildings, enclosed within more than a mile of 50-foot-tall sandstone walls. The emperor met daily with architects, builders and engineers to plan the enormous project.

Shah Jahan blended architectural ideas from many places to create the Taj Mahal complex. He used red sandstone, a traditional Hindustani building material. He used pointed arches and domes from Central Asia. And the garden, like the ones that Timur, and later Babur, had so lovingly created, was built in a style that had originated centuries before in Persia.

Shah Jahan wanted the 3,000-foot-long complex to be symmetrical, so that an imaginary center line would divide it into identical halves. He had the plans drawn over and over on paper marked with half-inch grid lines until the symmetry was perfect. When at last he was satisfied, he summoned the court astrologers. He may have been World Ruler, but he could not control the heavens. Construction could not start until the astrologers had studied the sun, moon, and stars and chosen a date that would guarantee success.

Shah Jahan summoned workers from all over the empire. Bricklayers, gardeners, stonemasons, and carpenters were among the thousands who flocked to the site. They were skilled and unskilled, men and women, Hindu and Muslim, and they all needed food, shelter, tools, and building materials.

Work animals—elephants and big-horned water buffalo—had to be tended, fed, and trained, adding to the confusion of the worksite.

A floating parade of heavily laden barges bearing wood, lime, and other building materials turned the Yamuna River into a construction highway. Carts rumbled along dusty roads carrying red sandstone from nearby quarries and marble from 200 miles away in Makrana.

Smoke from many fires drifted into the air over Agra as workers hardened mud bricks and burned lime to make mortar. Swarms of builders turned bricks, mortar, and rubble into garden walls and buildings.

Construction overseers were quick to strike with their long staffs to control the swirling activity and encourage cooperation. Despite the chaos, Hindustani building methods were fast and efficient.

The walls of the Taj Mahal complex were constructed by building two parallel brick walls and filling the space between with broken bricks and stone.

The thick walls were sturdy, but the brick and rubble construction was unsightly. It was the job of the Hindustani stonemasons to make them fit for a Mughal queen. They cut red sandstone into rectangular slabs which they attached securely to the walls with iron clamps. The stone slabs, carefully carved and smoothed, concealed the rough brick and gave the walls a beautiful face.

The stonemasons worked together in groups called guilds. Some guilds were members of the same family, others came from the same Hindustani village. Each guild included men and women, and each had its own history, skills, and techniques that older members had passed along to younger members for generations.

Guild members took pride in their skill and in the honor of working for the emperor. Some could not resist showing their pride by signing their work. They etched the symbol of their guild on the outside of the garden wall.

A stonemason (upper left) carves a flower, symbol of his guild, into the wall. Hundreds of different guild marks appear on the garden walls.

Mughal mausoleums were usually built at the exact center of a *charbagh*, but Shah Jahan had a different idea. He placed Mumtaz Mahal's tomb at the edge of the garden, overlooking the Yamuna River. It was an unusual decision, and a risky one. Every June and July when drenching monsoon rains swept across Hindustan, the Yamuna overflowed its banks. Perched at the river's edge, the Taj Mahal would be in danger of flooding. The builders had to devise ways to protect it.

Workers dug below the water line along the riverbank and built 1,000 wide, hollow brick columns that looked like wells. These "wells" were filled with broken bricks, limestone, and other rubble. The sturdy "wells" would support a huge brick and mortar plinth (platform) 1,000 feet long, 350 feet wide and 30 feet thick. The plinth would hold the Taj Mahal high above the flood.

The unruly Yamuna presented another challenge to the builders. They had to harness it as well as defend against it. Water was needed to irrigate the garden and fill its fountains, channels and pools. The river carried abundant cooling, life-giving water from the snowy Himalaya Mountains, but it was unpredictable. To ensure a dependable, year-round supply, the builders had to capture and store the river water.

Three large reservoir tanks were built on a high support outside the garden wall for storage. When water was needed, it was released into a sprawling grid of ceramic pipes buried beneath the garden. The pipes delivered water invisibly and effortlessly throughout the *charbagh*.

Moving water down from the storage tanks to the garden was easy enough—gravity did all the work—but moving it up from the Yamuna to the tanks was considerably harder. It had to be raised to a height of 50 feet and transported a distance of 900 feet. Many people and animals were required for that job.

An aqueduct was built atop high arches between the Yamuna and the reservoir tanks. Water buffalo did the work of raising water to the top of the aqueduct. From there the water flowed to the reservoir tanks.

a

The tank in the lower right hand corner holds water from the Yamuna. Workers standing in arched niches below the aqueduct scooped water from the tank into leather buckets. Each bucket was harnessed by a long rope to a water buffalo. When a bucket was full, a worker at the top of the aqueduct sent the water buffalo down a ramp on the far side. As the water buffalo walked down, the bucket was pulled up to be emptied into the aqueduct. When the big animal trudged back up the ramp, the empty bucket dropped down into the tank and the process began again.

Shah Jahan made another unusual architectural choice: he extended the Taj Mahal complex across the Yamuna. He built another garden, the Mahtab Bagh (Moonlight Garden), on the opposite bank. Shah Jahan lined up the Taj Mahal complex and the Mahtab Bagh so perfectly that their garden walls would have touched if there had been no river between them.

He built a marble viewing platform and reflecting pool at the edge of the Mahtab Bagh directly across the river from the mausoleum. Even before construction was finished, he and his courtiers could enjoy the scent of cypress trees and the cooling mist from fountains as they gazed at the Taj Mahal and its reflection.

From the viewing platform they could see the marble platform that sat in the center of the 1,000-foot-wide sandstone plinth. The platform lifted the Taj Mahal even higher, so that it was silhouetted dramatically against the sky. At each corner of the platform, a minaret tapered toward the sky. In the Muslim religion, only one minaret was needed, a tower from which the faithful were called to prayer, but Shah Jahan built four. He wanted to maintain the symmetry of his design. At the center of the platform, the unfinished Taj Mahal was rising, already a masterwork of soaring arches and domes.

The mausoleum, the four minarets, and the platform were strikingly different from the rest of the complex. Shah Jahan sheathed them in Makrana marble instead of red sandstone. The marble, faintly streaked in pale shades of gray and tan and white, has a unique quality. It appears to change color as the light changes from morning to evening, from sunlight to shadow. The Makrana marble was costly, but for Shah Jahan it was well worth the expense. This was the jewel of the burial complex, and he wanted it to gleam.

The words of Allah in black marble surround the mausoleum window (above). The pointed arch is decorated with colorful stone flowers. Even the window screen is made of stone—carefully carved Makrana marble.

Shah Jahan believed that he was creating a Paradise on earth for Mumtaz Mahal, and he showed that belief in many details. The octagonal shape of the mausoleum, for example, represented the eight levels of the Muslim Paradise. Passages from the Muslim holy book, the *Qu'ran*, that frame windows, doors, and gates throughout the complex speak beautifully of Paradise.

The flowing script, black marble inlaid into white, was the work of the gifted calligrapher Ahmanet Khan. He was the only person that Shah Jahan trusted to turn the sacred words of Allah into stone. The grateful emperor rewarded him richly with the gift of a valuable elephant. He even allowed him to sign his name in marble in the mausoleum, an extraordinary honor. Ahmanet Khan's is the only name that appears anywhere inside the walls of the Taj Mahal complex.

The first square of the Taj Mahal complex was an area of inns and markets called Mumtazabad (City of Mumtaz). Shah Jahan built it for the travelers who flocked to Agra to visit the famous tomb.

A visitor might have spent a restless night in busy, noisy Mumtazabad and in the morning been bumped and jostled by crowds pushing through the South Gate and into the Jilaukana (forecourt) toward the Great Gate, the only entrance to the charbagh.

At the Great Gate, an 11-story-tall building, the mood changed. From inside its towering archway, the visitor caught the first glimpse of the Taj Mahal. The sight of the gleaming pale dome floating, as if by magic, between the green of the gardens and the blue sky above, was enough to hush the most boisterous sightseer.

A few steps down, and the visitor was in the largest charbagh ever built. Like all Paradise gardens, Shah Jahan's was a perfect square, divided into four quarters by straight waterways. Spray from 73 fountains along the central waterway cooled the walk to the Taj Mahal. Rows of fruit trees and flower beds stretched to the distant garden walls.

At the top of the plinth, the visitor might have stopped at the mosque to pray, first washing hands and feet in the cleansing pool. A narrow flight of stairs led to the top of the marble platform. There, perhaps, the visitor might have walked to the edge to look out across the Yamuna to the Mahtab Bagh before turning back to enter the tomb of Mumtaz Mahal.

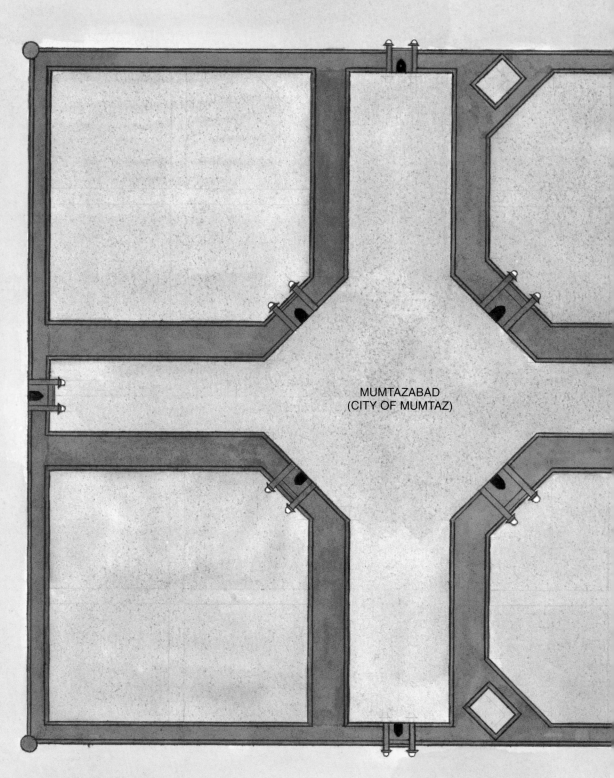

MUMTAZABAD
(CITY OF MUMTAZ)

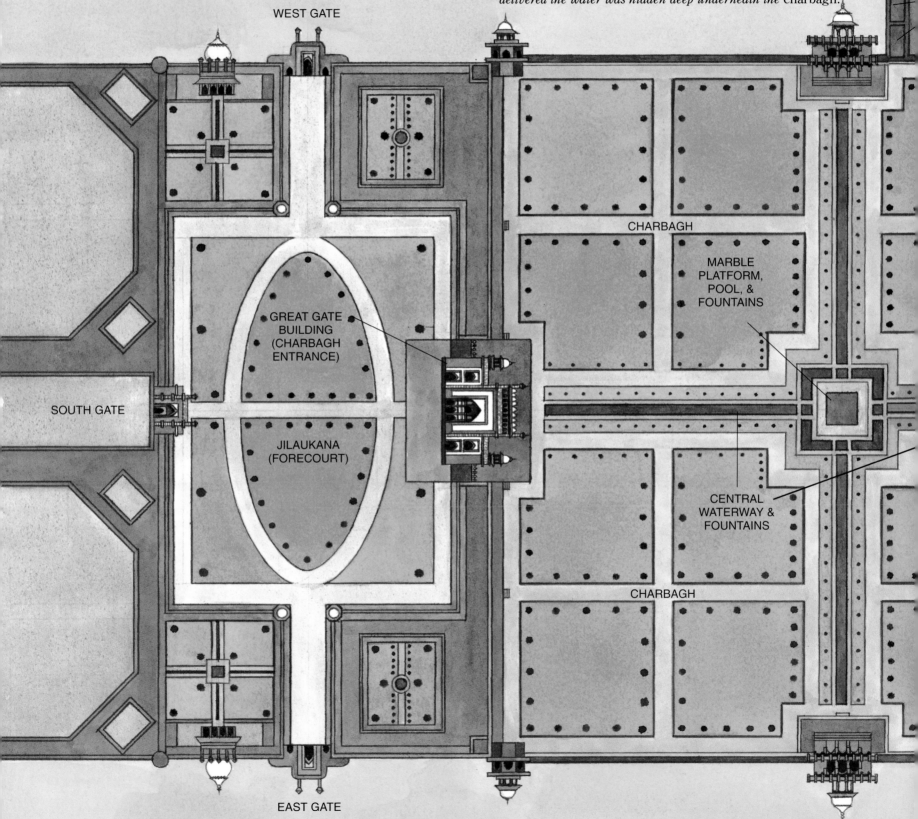

The aqueduct and reservoir tanks of the water system stood outside the garden walls, unseen by those who enjoyed the fountains and plants within. The network of clay pipes that delivered the water was hidden deep underneath the charbagh.

WEST GATE

CHARBAGH

MARBLE
PLATFORM,
POOL, &
FOUNTAINS

GREAT GATE
BUILDING
(CHARBAGH
ENTRANCE)

SOUTH GATE

JILAUKANA
(FORECOURT)

CENTRAL
WATERWAY &
FOUNTAINS

CHARBAGH

EAST GATE

The parchinkari *flower (above) is just inches across, but many tiny bits of semi-precious stone were meticulously shaped and embedded in the marble to create the fantastic detail. It is just one of many thousands that adorn Mumtaz Mahal's Paradise.*

In keeping with the Muslim religion, Shah Jahan used no images of people or animals in the Taj Mahal. Inside and out, he adorned the mausoleum with flowers. Like the flowers of Paradise, these would never wilt—they were made of stone.

Some were carved in raised relief on the marble. Others were made by setting bright gemstones into the marble, an art called *parchinkari*. Green jade from China, turquoise from the Himalaya Mountains, deep blue lapis lazuli from Central Asia were just a few of the many kinds of semi-precious stones that were transformed into brilliant blossoms and twisting vines. Against the translucent Makrana marble, the *parchinkari* flowers seemed lit from within.

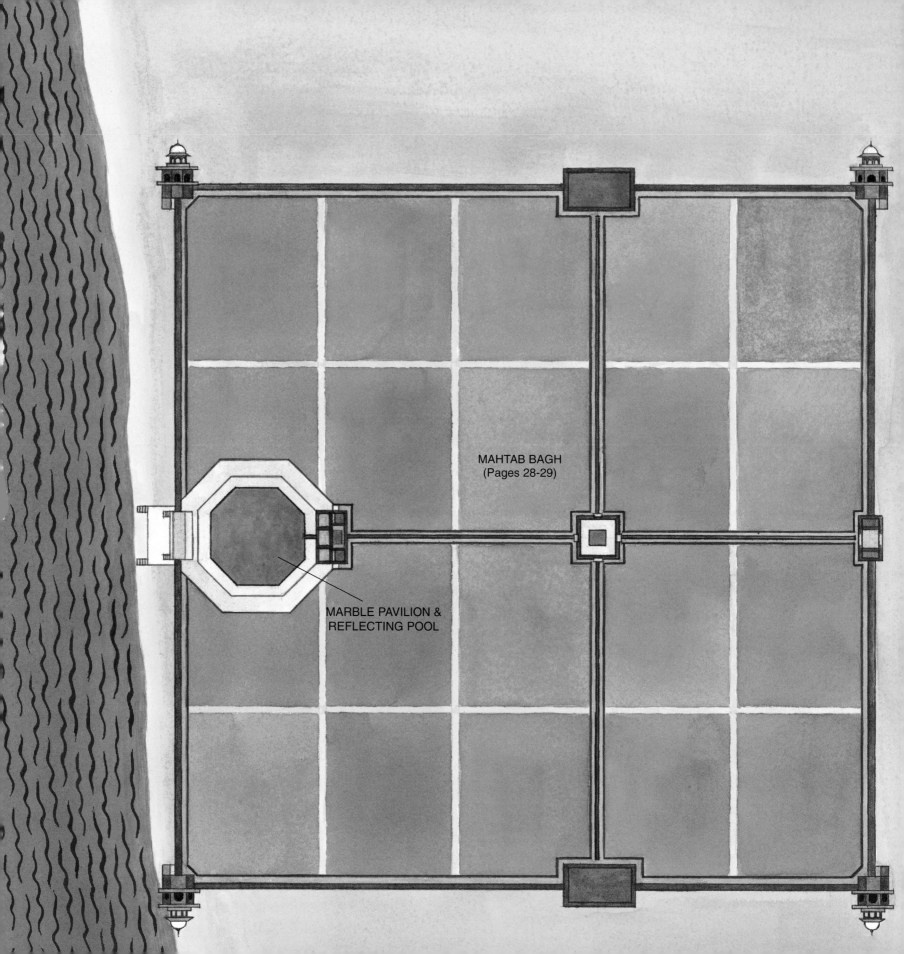

MAHTAB BAGH
(Pages 28-29)

MARBLE PAVILION &
REFLECTING POOL

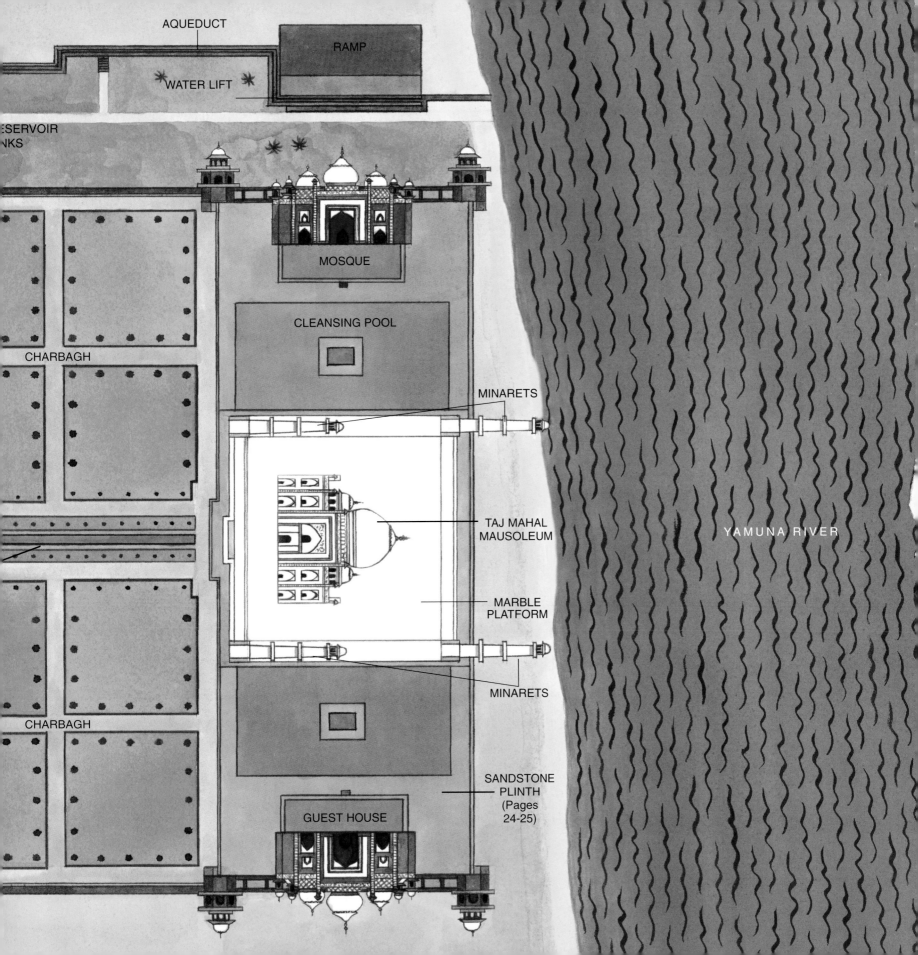

AQUEDUCT

RAMP

WATER LIFT

RESERVOIR
TANKS

MOSQUE

CHARBAGH

CLEANSING POOL

MINARETS

TAJ MAHAL
MAUSOLEUM

MARBLE
PLATFORM

MINARETS

CHARBAGH

SANDSTONE
PLINTH
(Pages
24-25)

GUEST HOUSE

YAMUNA RIVER

In 1638, before the Taj Mahal complex was finished, Shah Jahan made Delhi the capital of the empire. He had added so many nobles, advisors and attendants to his court that the palace in Agra could no longer contain them. In Delhi he built an enormous new city called Shahjahanabad (City of Shah Jahan). He moved his entire court up the Yamuna to Shahjahanabad and left the lovely Taj Mahal and its fragrant gardens for others to enjoy. Every year, though, he returned to Agra for the *urs*, the the anniversary of Mumtaz Mahal's death. In her name, Shah Jahan gave away gold and silver to thousands of poor people. In her honor, fireworks blazed above the Yamuna.

Shah Jahan had carefully planned every step of a visitor's walk through the complex, from Mumtazabad to the mausoleum, but it was not a walk he ever took. The emperor traveled instead by boat, reclining against silk pillows and cooled by river breezes.

He climbed stairs from the river's edge to the top of the marble platform, then stepped from the blinding sunlight into the cool dark of the Taj Mahal's main chamber. In the dim light filtered through the carved marble window screens, he could see the coffin-shaped cenotaph (burial monument) of cool white marble. The cenotaph marked Mumtaz Mahal's grave in the chamber directly below.

Sound hung in the air, captured by the echoing shape of the high domed ceiling. Stone flowers and vines wound across every surface. This was the Paradise that Shah Jahan had created for his queen.

In 1657, Shah Jahan fell ill. His four sons rushed to his side, but not to comfort him. In true Mughal fashion, each wanted to be ready to seize power if their father died. The emperor recovered from his illness, but his son Aurangzeb had already begun his own dreadful climb to power.

Shah Jahan wanted his favorite son, Dara Shukoh, to become emperor when he died, but Aurangzeb did not let that stand in his way. He had Dara Shukoh's head delivered to his father. It was a staggering move in Aurangzeb's campaign to eliminate competition for the throne, a campaign as brutal as his father's had been 30 years before.

Aurangzeb was even bolder than his father had been. Although Shah Jahan was still alive, he declared himself emperor. He stopped short of killing his father, and instead locked him in his palace in the Agra fort. The prisoner lived for seven years in his marble-walled jail, friendless and in failing health. He spent his days gazing out along the Yamuna River at the pale dome of the Taj Mahal, his proudest creation.

When Shah Jahan died in 1666, his body was moved quietly to the burial chamber beneath the Taj Mahal. It was placed next to Mumtaz Mahal's according to religious law: facing west toward the holy Muslim city of Mecca. Above, in the main chamber, a second white marble cenotaph was added to mark the new grave below. The two cenotaphs are there today, alive with *parchinkari* flowers, symbols of the undying flowers of the Muslim Paradise.

Shah Jahan's growing court, his vast building projects, his costly jewels drained Mughal wealth faster than his tax collectors could replenish it. The empire that Aurangzeb seized from his father in 1658 had begun a decline that would never be reversed. When he died in 1707, Aurangzeb was buried beneath a stone slab.

Mughal emperors ruled for another 82 years, but the time of greatness was over. The empire, and its rulers, grew weaker and weaker. Never again would a Mughal emperor aspire to create a Taj Mahal.

Today the Taj Mahal stands as the greatest achievement of an extraordinary people. It is a monument to the Mughal Empire, as well as to Shah Jahan and Mumtaz Mahal.

DATES

Chinghis Khan	ca. 1167-1227
Timur	1336-1405
Babur	1483-1530 (ruled 1526-1530)
Battle of Panipat	1526
Humayun	1508-1556 (ruled 1530-1540, 1555-1556)
Akbar	1542-1605 (ruled 1556-1605)
Jahangir	1569-1627 (ruled 1605-1627)
Shah Jahan born	1592-1666 (ruled 1628-1658)
Mumtaz Mahal born	1593
Shah Jahan and **Mumtaz Mahal married**	1612
Death of Mumtaz Mahal	1631
Taj Mahal built	1632-1643
Shah Jahan imprisoned	1658
Shah Jahan died	1666
Aurangzeb	1618-1707 (ruled 1658-1707)

FACTS

Mumtazabad— 1,000 feet wide x 1,100 feet long

Jilaukana—1,000 feet wide x 500 feet long

Charbagh—1,000 feet wide x 1,000 feet long

Plinth—1,000 feet wide x 375 long x 30 feet high

Marble platform—315 feet square x 20 feet high

Taj Mahal—186 feet square x 220 feet high

Minarets—140 feet high

Mahtab Bagh—1,000 feet wide x 750 feet long

Total Area of Taj Mahal Complex & Mahtab Bagh—95 acres

GLOSSARY

aqueduct—elevated water channel

cenotaph—burial monument

charbagh—square, high-walled, Persian-style garden

guild—workers' organization

Jilaukana—forecourt

Mahtab Bagh—Moonlight Garden

mausoleum—tomb building

minaret—tower from which Moslems are called to prayer

monsoon—heavy seasonal rains

mosque—Moslem place of worship

parchinkari—inlaid stone

plinth—sandstone platform supporting the Taj Mahal

Qu'ran—Moslem holy book (also spelled *Koran*)

urs—anniversary of a death

zanana—women's quarters

MAHAL BIBLIOGRAPHY

Asher, Catherine B., *Architecture of Mughal India*, (The New Cambridge History of India), Cambridge: Cambridge University Press, 1992.

Babur, Tr. Thackston, Wheeler M., *The Baburnama: Memoirs of Babur, Prince and Emperor,* Washington D.C: Freer Gallery of Art-Arthur M. Sackler Gallery, Smithsonian Institution, 1996.

Begley, W.E. & DeSai, Z.A, eds., *Taj Mahal: The Illumined Tomb, An Anthology of 17th Century Mughal and European Documentary Sources,* Cambridge, MA: The Aga Khan Program for Islamic Architecture, 1989.

Beach, Milo Cleveland, *King of the World: Padshahnama*, London: Azimuth Editions, Ltd. and Smithsonian Institution, 1997.

Gascoigne, Bamber, *The Great Moghuls,* New York: Dorset Press, 1971.

Havell, E. B.*, Indian Architecture Its Psychology, Structure, and History from the First Muhammedan Invasion to the Present Day*, London: John Murray, 1927.

Koch, Ebba, *The Compete Taj Mahal,* New York: Thames and Hudson, 2001.

Koch, Ebba, *Mughal Architecture: An Outline of Its History and Development,* New Delhi: Oxford, 2002 (1991)

Moynihan, Elizabeth B., *The Moonlight Garden,* Washington, D.C.: Arthur M. Sackler Gallery,: *Smithsonian Institution and Seattle: University of Washington Press, 2000.*

Moynihan, Elizabeth B., *Paradise As a Garden: In Persia and Mughal India,* New York: George Braziller, Inc., 1979.

Nath, R., *The Immortal Taj Mahal: The Evolution of the Tomb in Mughal Architecture,* D. B. Taraporevala Sons, 1972.

Nath, R., *Indigenous Characteristics of Mughal Architecture,* D K Printworld Pvt. Ltd., 2004.

Nath, R., *Mughal Inlay Art,* Delhi: Indian History and Culture Society, 2004.

Nou, Jean L., *The Taj Mahal,* New York: Abbeville, 1993.

Qaisar, Ahsan Jan, *Building Construction in Mughal India: The Evidence from Painting,* Delhi: Oxford University Press, 1988. (Center of Advanced Study in History, Aligarh Muslim University).

Richards, John F., *The Mughal Empire*, (The New Cambridge History of India), Cambridge: Cambridge University Press, 1993

Stronge, Susan, *Painting for the Mughal Emperor,* London: V & A Publications, 2002.

Wescoat, James L., Jr., (editor), *Mughal Gardens: Sources, Places, Representations, and Prospects,* Dumbarton Oaks Research Library and Collection, 1996.

Ziad, Zeenut, editor, *The Magnificent Mughals,* London: Oxford, 2002

PICTURE CREDITS:

INDEX

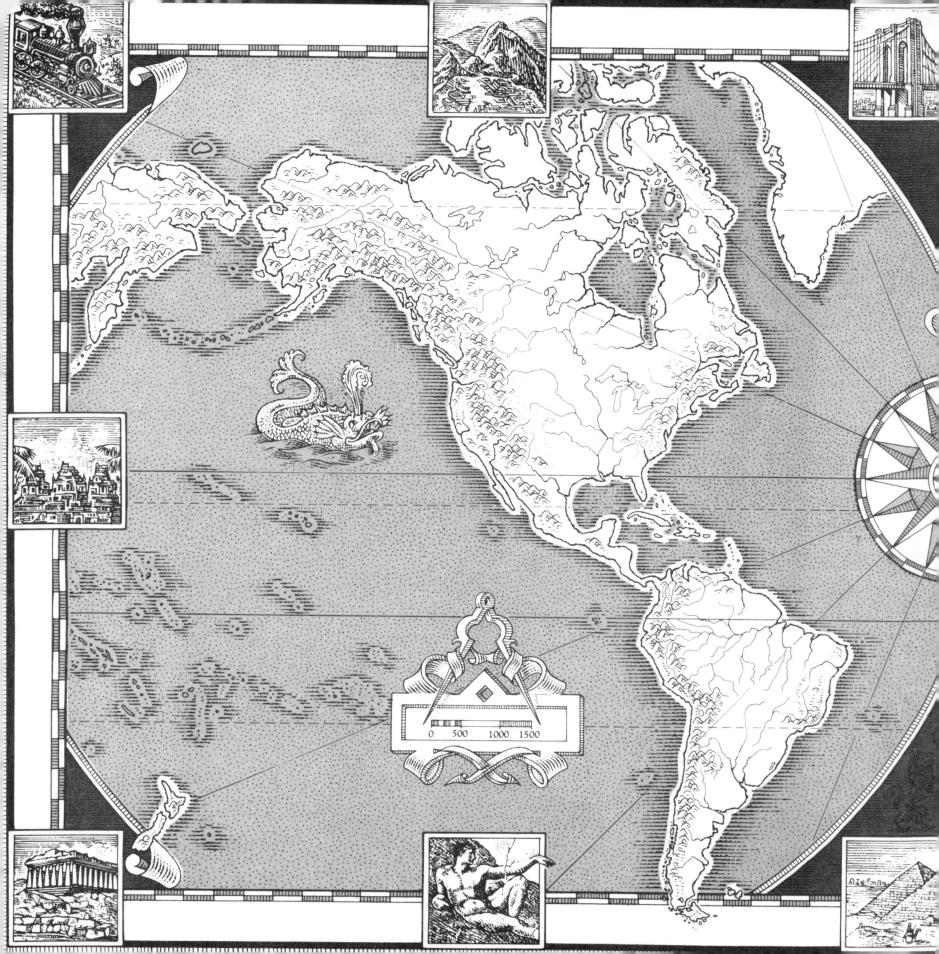

0 500 1000 1500